PAIDEIA MONOGRAPHS

THE DEVELOPMENT OF
CALVINISM
IN NORTH AMERICA

H. EVAN RUNNER

www.paideiapress.ca
www.reformationaldl.org

The Development of Calvinism in North America

This English monograph edition is a publication of Paideia Press (3248 Twenty First St., Jordan Station, Ontario, Canada L0R 1S0). Copyright ©2020 by Paideia Press. All rights reserved.

Except for brief quotations in critical publications or reviews, no part of this book may be reproduced in any manner without prior written permission from Paideia Press at the address above.

Unless otherwise indicated, Scripture quotations are from the ESV® Bible (The Holy Bible, English Standard Version®). Copyright © 2001 by Crossway, a publishing ministry of Good News Publishers. Used by permission. All rights reserved.

Paideia Monograph Series Editor: Steven R. Martins

Book Design by: Steven R. Martins

ISBN 978-0-88815-265-7

Printed in the United States of America

Contents

The Subject Matter & Method — 5

The European Background through the
Middle of the Seventeenth Century — 12

The Development of Calvinism in
North America — 51

About the Author — 63

THE DEVELOPMENT OF
CALVINISM
IN NORTH AMERICA

The Subject Matter & Method

THE ASSIGNED SUBJECT IS much too vast to be treated here in all its ramifications. We shall have to be selective. There is, however, more than one way to be selective. For our present subject we might decide to select a limited number of doctrinal questions and treat them in succession. For example, we might discuss first the fortunes of the doctrine of the covenant, and then the debate about predestination and free-will or the problem of infra- and supralapsarianism, and so on. The disadvantages of such a method are:

(1) that one has looked at certain aspects of Calvinism but at the same time has passed over others, thus acquiring only a partial perspective, or

probably no perspective at all;

(2) that one has missed the single *heart* of Calvinism.

A better selective treatment therefore would be to attempt to grasp the core-meaning of Calvinism and trace its fortunes here in the New World on the background of its fortunes in the Old. In this second way we can, in a sense, deal with the whole of our subject without having treated separately every one of its aspects.

This latter method commends itself since Calvinism is not a mere sum of theological positions. But then Calvinism has so very frequently been defined in a *theological* way that we had better say a word right here as to the sense in which we intend to employ the word. Perhaps the most vivid way to convey what I am driving at is to tell a short story.

I myself did not grow up in Calvinist circles although by a providential inconsistency I was required at a tender age to memorize the Shorter Catechism of the Westminster Assembly. In the Fundamentalist circles in which I grew up, anyone who believed in the perseverance of the saints and thereby denied that a genuine believer could fall away into final unbelief was considered to be a Calvinist. Later, through reading and contacts with movements more in the Reformed tradition, some of my friends and I came to feel that to be a Calvinist one must accept all of the "five points", i.e. the five articles against the *Remonstrants*, the so-called Canons of Dort, in English often schematically arranged under the letters of the word 'tulip', thus:

> T (otal Inability)
> U (nconditional Election)
> L (imited Atonement)
> I (rresistible Grace)
> P (erseverance of the Saints)

In this sense of the word there is an increasing group of "Calvinists" among fundamentalists of the U.S.A. Such people often accept the "five points" while rejecting the doctrine of the covenant and infant baptism. These two "additional" items I added to my personal arsenal while a student at Westminster Seminary in Philadelphia.

Of course, "Calvinism" existed long before the Remonstrant controversy and the ensuing formulation of the "points", else were Calvin no Calvinist. We may ask ourselves, What *led to* the formulation of these points? And the answer would run: The sense that Remonstrant teaching was endangering *Reformed religion*. The points were formulated to express what in Reformed religion was being threatened. But Reformed religion is the *prior possession!* Reformed religion, moreover, is nothing other than Biblical religion.

Calvinism is bound to the Scriptures. The faith of the Calvinist that in the Bible God addresses him is a faith effected in his heart by the Spirit of God. By that Spirit he is enabled to believe the fullness of Truth as that is concentrated in Jesus Christ, and thus to *stand* in the Truth. The fullness of Truth is one, not a collection of disparate or discrete items. We ought never to think that theological science pieces together for the first time into a systematic unity such a collection of discrete truths. Man's scientific thinking does not create this unity. As Prof. Mekkes says somewhere, every significance we attach to the various communications, pronouncements and commands is previously governed by our faith in this fullness of Truth, or better, is controlled by the hold this Truth takes of our heart. Scripture is the revelation of the Truth: in it we behold God in Christ reconciling the world unto Himself. As revelation of the fullness of Truth the Scripture sheds light upon reality in its entirety.

The Scripture speaks to us (1) of God the Creator, Who foreordains whatsoever comes to pass, i.e. of God the Sovereign over all; (2) of the Law of God in the all-encompassing sense of every word by which God subjects to His most holy Will all that He has made; (3) of the creation as wholly dependent upon the Creator, i.e. as completely subject to his law. Thus man too, in his state of original righteousness, was properly subject to the Law, mirrored the glory and righteousness of his Sovereign, and so was an image of God. Raised to covenant status, he was to walk *uprightly* before his God in the carrying out of his cultural task. This walk is religion. In the keeping of the Law was to be his great reward.

Further, Scripture speaks to us of the Fall and of Divine Redemption, i.e. of an antithetical *direction* in the life of man. Of fundamental discord and of the final victory of Christ's Kingdom of Righteousness.

Finally, Scripture tells us that God has made His people to be fellow-workers with Him in bringing in the Kingdom. We are said to be His witnesses. And as Dr. Vrieze writes in his brochure *Werker in een Nieuwe Wereld* (Church and Nation Series), p. 25f.:

> After all, (witnessing) is not only speaking, but also acting, submitting one's own actions to Christ's Word, but also seeking to put to work obedience to Christ's commandments, exerting such an influence that in social life there is a submission to that Word…

We need not despair when we see man resist the proclamation of the Word of God; for Christ has overcome the world. Men do not gradually come to agreement in this life; there is fundamental war. And there is no end to these woes until Christ returns in public victory and *puts down* His enemies. But in the meantime we have the consolation of which Prof. K.J. Popma writes:

> The Christ makes His own the second division of His army, of which He Himself is Captain and first division… He goes on, victorious, and takes His own in that victory… enables His own to form power. That is why it is always worth it, that is why it is worth our lives to found Christian schools, to pursue Christian politics and Christian social life, to stand for Christian science and Christian philosophy. That is worth everything: for sharing in the power-building of Christ makes all human work gleaming and glorious, in the midst of the pitifulness of our efforts, in the weakness of our enterprises and in the short-sightedness of our consultation. Here then is what we mean by Calvinism: Biblical religion, i.e. human life lived in the light of Biblical revelation, the walk of the believer before God, the carrying out in faith of Yahweh's mandate in accordance with the Law.

It was of some importance to show at the very outset that by Calvinism we mean, not, in the first place, certain more or less careful theological formulations of this or that point of doctrine, but a life lived in the light of the great religious realities we come to know by listening out of believing hearts to the Word of our God. For the judgments we make about the development of Calvinism will entirely depend on how we see Calvinism itself.

The committee was, in my opinion, very wise in suggesting that we consider the development of Calvinism in the New World on the background of its development in Europe. For, strictly speaking, there are no two developments. There is a widely accepted notion that American culture is profoundly different from European cultures. The one, it is frequently said, is young and vigorous; the other, old and withering. On this question I find myself in hearty agreement with the thesis of Prof. P. Sorokin of Harvard University, who some years ago now wrote:

> So far as the secondary characteristics of American and European cultures are concerned, there is no doubt but that they are different in many respects. But in regard to these secondary traits, no less different are the cultures of England and Italy, of France and Germany. Even different regions of the same country have many secondary differences in their culture. Even various social classes and groups of the same region, the same city, or the same town differ from one another in hundreds of cultural traits. The problem concerns not these secondary differences but the essential characteristics of both

European and American cultures. When the question is put in that form, the answer is that *in spite of some three or four centuries of geographical separation, there has been for a long time and still is, only one culture, the Western or Euro-American culture, identical on both continents in all its essential traits. Being essentially identical, it is of the same age on both continents, not a bit younger in America than in Europe. As such, it changes along similar lines on both continents, and passes in this change through the same main phases and exhibits similar tendencies. So it was during the seventeenth and eighteenth centuries, and has continued to be up to the present time.*"

What Sorokin says in general is true in particular of the development of Calvinism. We shall begin therefore by saying something about the European development of Calvinism up through the middle of the seventeenth century. Before 1620, and radically before the end of the mighty emigration to the Massachusetts Bay Colony (1630-40) one can scarcely speak of development in America.

The European Background through the Middle of the Seventeenth Century

A. The Reformation and the Basic (Religious) Problem of Unity, Unanimity, Concord, Peace, Order in Human Society

Concord and Unity are a matter of religion. When

God opens the hearts of men to give heed to His Will, a unanimity or oneness of heart (Greek, *homonoia*; Latin, *concordia*) results: the will to do the Father's Will. The unity of men is achieved in their single-hearted devotion to God. Thus, unity has of necessity a super-temporal origin in the Kingdom of God: the mind of Christ the Head is formed in the members of the body.

To be sure, no pagan thinkers of ancient times had had such an insight into the relation between our total temporal life and the pre-temporal root in the religious relation to God and His Law. But ancient writers like Aristotle and Cicero had realized that a truly stable society is impossible where there is dissension or discord, not, of course, about trivial matters, but about ultimates, specifically, about the supreme or ultimate authority or power in society. In the words of the contemporary Spanish philosopher Jose Ortega y Gasset, "Concord implies a firm and common belief regarding the exercise of supreme power." In the State, which to the ancients was the all-encompassing bond of society, there had to be agreement on fundamentals, and such agreement was guaranteed by religious sanction. Various Olympian deities sealed the authority of the several Greek city-states; the old Roman religion secured a common belief in the authority of the Republic.

When the common belief is lacking a crisis of the foundations ensues. Such a crisis arose in the time of Cicero: belief in the old religion of the Romans was gone, and with it the basis for stability in the life of the State itself. What happens in a society when a firm and common belief in the ultimate sovereignty has been lost? Cicero asked himself the Question. Society requires the executive function. Lacking a genuine solution, she resorts to a *makeshift*. Such a makeshift was the Roman Empire. A balance of forces.

By pointing to the sole supremacy of the Word of God the Reformation put an end to any commonness of faith that yet existed in Europe as to the ultimate authority. That meant that the basis of the medieval order of Church and Empire was gone. Since almost all men of the time were committed to the axiom that there had to be agreement on fundamentals if there were to be a stable society, we can understand the bitter struggles that took place between the forces of the Reformation and the Roman Church and Empire. Each group, convinced of the truth of its position, was out to gain the common consent of Europeans. When this proved impossible, the result was another makeshift: the *Religious Peace of Augsburg of 1555*, by which the Lutheran religion was given legal status within the Empire. The principle of *cuius regio eius religio* was recognized, and subjects were granted the privilege of emigrating without molestation. This makeshift accentuated the local autonomy of the princes and contributed to the further breakdown of the Empire.

Men who thought fundamentally about the European situation realized that a mechanical balance of forces was not the solution to the question of European stability. Moreover, the Calvinists, who had rapidly increased in number and counted many energetic leaders in a number of important towns, were not recognized in the "solution" by 1555. The Wars of Religion which broke out were followed by the *Peace of Westphalia of 1648*. This treaty confirmed the Religious Peace of Augsburg of 1555 and extended its provisions to the Reformed Churches. Toleration was now secured for the three great religious communities of the "Empire". Within these limits the governments were bound to allow at least private worship, liberty of conscience, and the right of emigration.

The *Peace of Westphalia* remained the basis of European public law until the outbreak of the French Revolution, when a thoroughly secular view of the basis of society became culturally dominant. The toleration granted by the treaty of 1648 was of the old kind, but henceforth persecution, even of groups not recognized in the treaty, was the exception rather than the rule. A principal reason for this tolerant execution of its provisions was that almost imperceptibly men's minds had been growing more tolerant. This tolerance was the expression of a new outlook on the world which was rapidly winning followers, especially among cultural leaders, in the early decades of the seventeenth century.

Let us take a brief look at this new outlook.

B. The 'Modern' View of Unity, Peace and Concord

In the new mind that was beginning to become perceptible in Europe, tolerance was opposed to dogmatism. So, at least, it was thought. In the writings of many one can feel the deep distaste for the passions that were exhibited in the religious wars, the sensing that things cannot go on in this way. Unquestionably there comes a weariness of spirit, a deep longing for peace and concord, such as the Middle Ages had enjoyed. Of course, the unanimity of belief that had given divine sanction, in the earlier Middle Ages to both Emperor and Pope, in the later period (think of Popes Gregory VII, Innocent III, Boniface VIII) to the Emperor *through* the Pope – that faith was no longer shared commonly by Europeans. But just because they were weary, men were not inclined to be indifferent. This was an age of great cultural development and hope. No, it was not a spirit of indifference to religion that was making itself felt in the new spirit of tolerance in those middle years of the seventeenth century. It was something more positive than that. Men were seeking a *new basis for unity*.

That new basis must not be something that comes to man from without. It must come from within man himself, must be something *natural*, something in his nature. We can see this new mind already in that Humanistic movement of the Italian Renaissance that we know as the Florentine Academy. From there it went to France and thence to all of Europe. Sometimes it attached to the Neoplatonists of the third century of our era; sometimes, to the ancient Stoics. Men were becoming fascinated with Nature itself, especially with human nature, and with what in the latter was called *Reason*. I am speaking of the movement we know as Rationalism.

What is rationalism? Here we have one of those big words that are so difficult to define because they cover such a wide range of opinions. However, in general we may say that it means that men are impressed with the *clarity*, *authority*, and *universal acceptability* of Nature and Nature's laws, the laws of Reason. You ask what reason means to these men and I find it hard to say. The rationalists hardly raise the question. The common assumption is that everybody knows. But the idea is that in the nature of every man there is, not merely an ability to think, to analyze, but, in addition, an ascertainable outfit of intellectual, moral and religious convictions *the validity of which is a matter of universal agreement*. Reason is the deepest core of man, and reason is everywhere and always the same. At the time this seemed axiomatic.

Here we feel the religious motive at work in the sudden spread of rationalism. The "unity" of society had been as good as destroyed. On the basis of Reformed religion, viz. that unity comes only from our common, single-hearted service of God in obedience to His law, unity was not to be achieved. Leibniz, one of the greatest thinkers of the age, tried all his life to find a basis for the reunion of the several Christian communities, but to no avail. It was beginning to become clear than an order of universal agreement, so necessary for a stable society, could no longer be based upon confession of Christian dogma. To many leading thinkers therefore it appeared that if there was to be a really universal system of law, ethics, or religion that it would have to be based upon such principles as could be readily acknowledged by every nation, creed and sect. Just such principles are now asserted, quite dogmatically it would seem, to be the *a priori* possession of every man! (*A priori* simply means: prior to every particular experience and making these possible.)

Thus man returned to an ancient view, *that man has*

within his very being the law for his jural, ethical, and religious life, to mention only the areas most prominently in discussion at the time. Natural religion, natural morality and natural law are simply three aspects of the one situation.

The new outlook is conspicuously anti-Christian, although many men who considered themselves Christian had to do with its development. For one thing, it denies that our lives are normed by something outside us, the will of the Sovereign Creator, under whose judgment we stand. The law is now nothing other than the outfit of *a priori* ideas of our Reason, our own deepest *self*. There is no room for transgression. Man is not seen as a servant of God; he is seen by himself. In human life therefore there is no antithesis.

In the year of the treaty of Westphalia (1648), a man died who may be said to have ushered in one phase of the new thinking, Deism. I refer to the Englishman Edward Herbert, Lord Herbert of Cherbury (1583-1648), whose famous book *De Veritate* (On Truth) was published in 1624. Like the other men of this new movement Herbert professed to make a radical break with all past philosophizing, and to set out upon a new and necessary course. He believes that a way can be found to escape the raging conflict of opinions and arrive at areas of basic agreement. He straightway warns his readers that he proposes to deal, not with religion, but with the understanding. Yet there are verities of religion which the understanding accepts. For in the understanding the Natural Instinct reveals to us certain Common Notions, notions common to all mankind. He cites two such Common Notions, religion and law, and, though he admits that there are various religions and various laws, the problem is *to find the primordial ideas shared by all mankind, and on them to erect a universal religion and a universal law.* In this task Herbert's *belief*(!) is that a real antithesis or basic contradiction does not exist since men could not be so at variance with one another and still be men.

Note that Herbert does not prove an area of agreement; he assumes it, on the ground that (in spite of the experience of the early seventeenth century!) the opposite is inconceivable. Note too that he fails to distinguish with Scripture between the *structure* and the *direction* of our lives, and thus arrives at a view completely in conflict with the Christian religion, viz. the denial of the antithesis in the *direction* of human life. The Common Notions are said to maintain the order and stability of the Cosmos. This is the function, in reality, of the law of God, but to Herbert the Notions are in our nature and are understood in and of themselves. They are inscribed within us by *Nature*; they are "not so much the outcome of experience as principles without which we should have no experience at all." That is to say that they are legislative for our experience; they are the law for experience. This is what is meant by calling them innate. They are universal and necessary. They are *a priori*.

As to religion there are, according to Herbert, five points of "natural" religion: (1) there is a Supreme Power; (2) it is our duty to worship that Power; (3) the practice of virtue (natural morality) is part of the worship which men render to God; (4) impiety and crime are expiated by penitence; (5) reward and punishment await us in the life to come. In these five points we have the essence of all religion, and of all historical faiths. The differences are only in the trappings. *Here we see the basic reason for the new mind of tolerance.* What is there to get excited about? In essence the various religious parties do not differ. Each is saying the same thing, but in a different key. Christianity is merely a re-publication of that essential religion which is as old as the Creation!

The next year (1625) – Herbert's *De Veritate* appeared in 1624 – another book of major importance for the new mentality appeared, the *De Jure belli et pacis* (Law of War and Peace) of Huig de Groot (Hugo Grotius). Here again we hear of a universally valid Law which Nature has graven on the hearts of men. Grotius, one of the Remonstrants, you will remember – he therefore considered himself a Christian –, who is also known for his exposition of the governmental theory of the atonement, expressed himself extremely cautiously. He was himself, he said, a Christian and accepted the Law of God, but for the public life of Europe a more universally acceptable basis of law must be found, and that he took to be the Law of Nature, indelibly engraved upon every man's heart. On the basis of certain primordial ideas of Law Grotius builds his contribution to international law, a law of our nature that holds in time of war when civil law does not.

Two laws: the law of God and the Law of Nature. Grotius, of course, had not first found out this twofold formula. Indeed, it can be found in Thomas Aquinas, the classic spokesman of Roman Catholic thought. It runs through all the later Middle Ages. What then was new about it that would cause it to be criticized and condemned by the ecclesiastical authorities? Why the sudden furor? In the words of the great French historian of ideas, Paul Hazard:

> Its novelty lay in the patent separation of the two terms; in the no less evident tendency to stretch their opposition; and then in an attempt to reconcile the two, which of itself implied that the rift was a real one. Above all, it

THE DEVELOPMENT OF CALVINISM IN N.AMERICA | 23

lay in an idea – which, though not as yet clearly defined, was full of vigor: War, violence, disorder, which the law of God does not repress but suffers rather, and even justifies, as being part of an inscrutable design, all the ills which man is heir to – perhaps the day will come when some human law will bring about their mitigation, their abolition. Thus we are invited, with manifold excuses for such boldness, to pass from the Order of Providence to the Order of Humanity.

Some years later (1672-73) Samuel Pufendorf, a German legal theorist teaching at the Swedish University of Lund, wrote two books that were in Grotius' line. He granted that there is a divine power or plane of revelation, but he asserted that there is also a plane of natural law and moral theology (Reason). The former plane is said to be concerned with Heaven; the latter, with this earth. What is so startling is the comfortable way Pufendorf has of confining his human interest entirely to the earth. The danger was felt by the Swedish pastors, and the professor was set upon.

One could go on for a long time. Let the above suffice to show that the new outlook was nothing less than an alternative answer to the fundamental religious questions of man's life, the question of unity and concord, the question of the Law, etc. As such an alternative to Reformed religion it was, of course, antithetical to Reformed religion. Although sometimes cautiously formulated, the new view looked upon man, not as a religious being, whose meaning can only be sensed in his (covenantal) relation to God and His Law, but as a rational-moral being, i.e. a being who has *within himself*, in his very structure, quite apart from how he stands before God, the Law and the Gospel, a right reason, i.e. a proper guide to life, a true knowledge of the Law and an ability to act in conformity with this knowledge.

The new age was an age of belief in the *normalcy* of man. Such men did not hesitate to leave Revelation and the Kingdom of Christ to the private lives of those who showed some concern for these matters. They themselves, on the other hand, ignoring what they thought of as

> metaphysical chimeras that had always led mankind astray", sought, by concentrating on the appearances that are within their grasp, "a political system without divine sanction (the social contract – H.E.R.), a religion without mystery, a morality without dogma.

These were the men who took up with unfailing confidence the building of the Kingdom of Man on Earth. Communism is one form of the general pattern. In later days these men took on the industrial and technological revolutions in their all-consuming passion to find happiness by their own efforts.

THE DEVELOPMENT OF CALVINISM IN N.AMERICA | 25

C. The Development of Calvinism in Europe through the Middle of the 17th Century

In a Europe undergoing such profound change, what were the fortunes of Calvinism? This is the question to which we must now turn. In doing so we must always keep before us a lively picture of the one great basic issue: What is man? For Reformed religion, as we have seen, man is in no way a unit closed off in himself. He was *put* here by God to image, in the creation, the divine glory. He was put here as God's vice-regent, to carry out the divine assignment (cultural mandate) in accordance with the Will (Law) of God. In other words, in his existence, taken concretely, man is a being who everywhere and in all things stands *in relation to God*. This relation is not true of merely a part of man. Man as a *whole* is heart, a religious being, made for covenant fellowship with Yahweh. Only when man in the *Totality* of his being is seen in this ultimate religious relation to God is he seen as he *is*. This scriptural revelation about man sheds light on what is *central* and *integral* in him.

The purity of this scriptural revelation about man was lost when in the Middle Ages an attempt was made to *accommodate* Christianity to the thought-results of the ancient Greeks, first, by agreeing to the pagan view of man as 'a being endowed with reason', and then by attempting to preserve the Christian revelation by adding to that that man is also a religious or *believing* being. (Here we have the famous medieval problem concerning faith *and* reason.) For then man is first taken as having a being *in himself* (reason) after which the *religious relation* is seen as something that was added to the essence (*donum superadditum*). (Cf. the Roman Catholic view of apostasy as the *lack* of the *donum superadditum*.) In such a view the meaning of Scripture is no longer grasped. For in Scripture the relation to God determines the *essence* of man, what man precisely is in his concrete totality. Prof. Berkouwer in his book, *Man the Image of God*, therefore rightly speaks of such a view of man as "*the antithesis of what we can call the biblical view of man*" (p. 31). Yet how often in our immediate circles we hear man *defined* as a rational-moral being!

In the medieval view ancient paganism was preserved as a distinct area or sphere *unreformed* by Biblical revelation, the so-called realm of *Nature* (and Natural Reason). To it was added the area of special revelation, of grace and faith, the so-called realm of *Grace*. So we arrive at the *scheme of Nature and Grace*. This scheme is simply an attempt to hold on to the results of paganistic reflection (i.e. reflection without benefit of the light of God's Word) and add to them the light of special revelation. In that way, however, the true nature of special or word-revelation is misconstrued. For in asserting natural reason to be a light in the lower realm it denies that Scripture is the *only* light (illumination) we have in our spiritual darkness (2 Pet. 1:19; cf. Rom. 1:21; John 1:5). As soon as Christian scholasticism (this medieval view) thought it had found a real, autonomous starting-point in the *ratio* (the Latin word for Reason) of the natural sphere (*ratio naturalis*) the destruction of Christianity itself could no longer be checked.

Yet this scheme of Nature and Grace, or of Nature and Supranature (that which is above, in addition to, Nature) was the underling governing motive of thinkers in Christian circles for centuries, and even the Reformation, from the beginning, failed to overcome it.

Luther, we realize today better than ever before, had seen the meaning of Biblical religion as a *coram Deo vivere*, i.e. a life before God's face, out of faith.[1] Nevertheless, the traces of the scheme of Nature and Grace, as that was conceived by William of Occam and Gabriel Biel, are not to be denied. Eg. the opposition

---

1. Cf. diss. 'J. Bakker, *Coram Deo*, Kok 1956, and H.R. Gerstenkorn, *Woltlich Regiment Zwischen Gottesreich und Teufelsmacht*, Bonn, 1956. The latter was reviewed by Prof. Mekkes in *Philosophia Reformata*, 22e jrg. 2o kw. blz. 95f).

of law and gospel. And the willingness to leave the government of the churches to the "secular" princes.

In Calvin also, however much it may be in conflict with the fundamental structure of his thought, it is not difficult to find traces of the scheme of nature and supranature.[2]

But there was especially one matter which seemed to work much for the maintaining of the scheme of Nature and Grace in the Protestant world. I am speaking of the doctrine of a *natural law*, which we met in Grotius and which is unquestionably one of the principal historical factors in the formation of the modern spirit. The ancient Stoics, in connection with their teaching about a universal agreement (brotherhood) of men, had developed a *ius gentium* (law of nations) and, as underlying that, a *ius naturale* (natural laws), a common fund of moral ideas. On that basis Seneca, in his *De Clementia*, had warned the Emperor Nero that even the tyrant is subject to certain commonly recognized principles of conduct.[3] Through its great influence upon Neoplatonism Stoical ideas entered the Church Fathers and became a part of scholastic philosophy,

---

2. Cf. *Institutes*, II:2, 13ff.
3. Cf. the purpose of Grotius' book, and Calvin's intention in addressing Francis I in his commentary on Seneca's *De Clementia*.

and of canon and civil law. The idea of a natural law and of an original contract was used by the Conciliarists in their struggle against the Curialists at the end of the Middle Ages. The Humanist movement revived Neoplatonic thought and Stoical theory. The idea of a 'right reason' was very much a part of the Humanist movement in which Calvin and Melanchthon were educated. In this connection it is interesting to read the statement of August Lang in his often overlooked but exceedingly rewarding article "The Reformation and Natural Law" in the anniversary volume *Calvin and the Reformation*, Revell, 1909, who writes that there are no indications that *all* the Reformers "held *as a matter of learned tradition* some kind of conception of a specific natural law. But in distinction from Melanchthon, Luther attributed to it only a subordinate importance, Calvin almost no importance at all" (p. 71f., italics mine). That could mean that natural law was in these men more of a remnant, not yet "judged" in the light of Reformation teaching.

The case of Melanchthon, about whom the debate still goes on as to whether he built up or tore down Luther's evangelical work, is different from the others and highly instructive. Already in the first edition (1521) of his *Loci Communes*, the first Protestant systematic theology, he inserts a section on natural law (*lex naturae* or *ius naturale*) with an appendix on the law of nations (*ius gentium*). In Rom. 2:15 Melanchthon finds a Biblical attestation of this law of nature with its innate moral principles. Yet the Fall has darkened human reason, and while the moral faculty survives, the content of the innate moral law can scarcely be disengaged from the corruptions that have intruded themselves. Somewhat later, however, Melanchthon "turned aside towards synergism." Synergism is the view that *alongside* the Word of God and the Holy Spirit the human will is to be placed as one of the cooperating principles in conversion. It grants thus to something in man an independence from the religious situation in which man as a totality finds himself. Lodged somewhere within man's nature there is something that is normal (not involved in the apostasy from the service of God with the whole heart) on that it recognizes what is right and proper. In that light it is significant that in the editions of the *Loci* subsequent o 1535, after Melanchthon had embraced this unevangelical view, his disposition to natural law, reason and the moral faculty are much more favourable. So much so that a recent German study on Melanchthon's *Doctrine of Natural Law* concludes that the final version of the *Loci*

> contains a fully developed theory of natural law, which is presented as an organic component of Melanch-

thon's whole theological doctrinal structure. Something which is really outside this structure has now become an integral part of it.[4]

It is outside this structure because it abstracts from the total man, who is in a state of religious apostasy,[5] something which then just *is* (there). The question of normal or abnormal is not even raised: that would require an ultimate relation to a Norm-coming-from-without. Natural law is something that arose in a pagan environment, where man just *is*, a rational substance, with the Law in himself, and where, out of considerations of self-interest he makes a transition from a natural state to a civil state by means of a social contract, which is succeeded, in turn, by a governmental contract between the civil parties.

In Reformed circles too, as early as the sixteenth century, we suddenly find natural law theories everywhere. In France, in order to attain a firm legal foundation for resistance against a hostile government, the Monarcho-machists grasped at the conception of a natural law.[6] Important it is to know that Languet

---

4. Clemens Bauer, in *Archiv fur Reformations– geschichte*, XLII (1951), 64-100.
5   Cf. Melanchthon's handling of natural law in the first edition of 1521.
6. E.g. Hubert Languet in *Vindiciae contra Tyrannes*, 1579 and

was so impressed by the *Loci* of Melanchthon, which he read while studying law in Padua and Bologna, that he traveled Wittenberg and remained with Melanchthon twelve years, until that man's death in 1560. Later Languet was in the service of William of Orange. Consider what he has to say of natural law:

> The Law is reason and wisdom itself, free from all perturbation, not subject to be moved with choler, ambition, hate, or acceptances of persons… To come to our purpose, the law is an understanding mind, or rather the manifold of understanding minds in its unity: the mind being the seal of all the intelligent faculties, is (if I may so term it) a parcel of divinity; in so much as he who obeys the law, seems to obey God, and receives Him for arbitrator of the matters in controversy.

Not only in France, but also in Scotland we find these ideas. In the same year as the *Vindiciae*, there was published the *Dejure regni apud Scotos* of the Scottish poet and scholar, George Buchanan, whose life had been largely spent in France. In this book, which curiously was written for the author's royal pupil, the future James I of England, we find a rather clear statement of the ancient Stoic view that the government originates in the social propensities of men and is therefore nat-

---

Francois Hotman in *Francogallia*, 1573).

ural. In this respect Buchanan tended to minimize the dependence of politics upon revelation.

In England, in Richard Hooker's *Of the Laws of Ecclesiastical Polity Eight Books*, the first five books of which appeared before the close of the sixteenth century, we behold an Anglican defending his practices against the Puritan doctrine that nothing may be allowed in the church that is not expressly taught in Scripture. First, he limits the authority of Scripture:

> he holds that human aids are indispensable for the purpose of determining what Scripture teaches. The Scripture is indeed the foundation of all things, but the authority of man is the key that unlocks its meaning. Nor did the opposing party, Hooker claims, have any better right to say that their teaching was the pure truth of God, they too depended in their interpretation of Scripture upon human opinion.[7]

Finally, Hooker takes refuge in the law of reason and nature.

> Even in matters of revelation we cannot do without the reason; only rational reflection can make us certain what God's word is. The *testimonium spiritus sancti internum* is not sufficient to insure the authority of the Word; for the operations of the Spirit are by their na-

---

7. Lang, "The Reformation and Natural Law", 78.

ture obscure and must be tested by the reason before their genuineness can be settled… we obtain something useful only from Scripture and reason together.

Man has within himself a law of reason, which in every individual case points out what is good, and that, too, with compelling force, so that it must be done. This law of reason corresponds to the operations of nature, it is the law of nature. In it the moral faculty of man finds expression, and it is therefore universally valid; to it the positive laws, which owe their origin to definite legislative acts, whether of a human state or of God, stand related as regulations that cannot be obligatory for ever. Among the latter Hooker includes certain 'supernatural duties.' The law of nature as the natural light of reason does not, it is true, embrace all necessary laws; above all, it cannot be kept without the continual help and cooperation of God; but still it can be recognized without the assistance of Revelation.[8]

We begin to see how it was possible for Archbishop Tillotson in the seventeenth century to say, "All the duties of Christian religion which respect God, are no other but what natural light prompts men to, excepting the two sacraments, and praying to God in the name and by the mediation of Christ." Religion was coming

---

8. Ibid., 78f.

more and more to rest upon 'Nature.' Even the orthodox, who retained the supernatural basis, felt that fate must be grounded firmly upon Nature before one had recourse to Supranature. Whereas Nature formerly was thought of as preparing for Revelation, now Nature was beginning to furnish the principal evidences of religion, while a somewhat embarrassing Revelation must be harmonized with it as best might be. It was too great a step from Tillotson to Anthony Collins, who, in his *Discourse of Freethinking* (1713), after quoting the words of Tillotson we have just cited, says of Tillotson's exceptions: "And even these are of less moment than any of those parts of religion which in their own nature tend to the Happiness of human Society."

We have just about arrived at the Remonstrant in Holland, Hugo Grotius, of whom we have already spoken earlier. Well we may ask ourselves how it was possible that such a development could take place. Lang explains it chiefly by "the compulsion of circumstances."[9] Permit me to quote him at some length.

> The Reformation at its very beginning found itself in the presence of problems and exigencies of indefinite range, first of all, conflicts of purely religious and theological character – doctrinal, liturgical, and constitution-

---

9. Ibid., 94.

al conflicts. What an amount of spiritual strength was consumed even by these conflicts! How much there was which went wrong! What unrest, what losses these conflicts produced! And yet the problems which then appeared could be settled by reference to the fundamental religious principle of Protestantism, and on the whole were in fact settled in a truly Protestant way. Much more difficult and dangerous, however, was a second adjustment, which lay more on the periphery of religious truth and yet was no less necessary – namely, the adjustment to the general ethical, political and social problems, to science and art. This adjustment, I say, was unavoidable for if Protestantism over against the Medieval-Catholic world, involves a new world-view, then there must necessarily be a Protestant science of Politics, a Protestant philosophy and science, a Protestant art…

For such an adjustment, however, in the very nature of things time is required; it cannot be accomplished by one man or by one generation… But now the tasks and problems of culture came upon the young evangelical Church in a storm… What was needed – firm principles about the relation of the Reformation to the forces of culture – to the state, science and art – was lacking and how could it be attained all at once in the midst of all the unrest of the time? Regarded in this way, we believe, the appearance of natural law becomes comprehensible. A doctrine of the state constructed on evangelical principles was not in existence. But such a doctrine was imperatively demanded by the need of the time. Men needed to have clearness about the relation of the ruler to the subjects, about the problem of Church and state, about the relation between different churches in the same country. No wonder that in the lack of a conception of the state revised in the light of fundamental evangelical ideas, men had recourse to the political theory taught in the traditional jurisprudence, without heeding the fact that that theory had an origin foreign to the Reformation and involved tendencies and consequences which would lead away from the Reformation. These tendencies, of course, became apparent later in slowly-developing after-effects, and then, especially after the spiritual enervation sustained in the protracted religious wars, they could not fall gradually to dissipate and destroy the Reformation's basis of faith.

Unless all indications are deceptive, the progress of events was similar in the case of other cultural questions. The desire for knowledge, the desire for activity, which was experienced by the individual after he had been liberated through the Reformation, plunged itself into all problems of the spiritual life of man, *became absorbed in the traditional manner of their treatment*, and was all too quickly satisfied with solutions which were not in agreement with the fundamental ethico-religious factors of the practical religious life of the Reformation. The reaction did not remain absent. The evangelical life of faith became shallower, instead of deepening itself and developing all directions."[10]

Indeed, many factors were at work in the sixteenth century to fix men's attention, and even their hopes, upon what was called Reason. There was, first, the fact that Rome continued to attack the Protestants with the weapons of scholastic philosophy, Aristotle's *Metaphysics* in the first place. If protestant leaders were to meet e.g. Suarez's arguments, they would, it seemed, have to be just as skillful as he in the use of the same weapons.

Second, the doctrinal debates between the later, scholastic Lutherans and the Reformed theologians required an ever more refined subtlety in the use of the syllogisms and metaphysical distinctions of Aristotle. This concentration upon close reasoning led men to acquire an inordinate respect for logic and what was called Reason. The Reformed religion began to turn into an academic exegesis of "theological" reasoning.

---

10. It might prove illuminating, in connection with the above quotation, to read what A. Kuyper wrote as *Voorwoord* to his three-volume *De Gemeene Gratie*. I have quoted it in my *The Christian and the World* and in *Cui Bono*.

Calvinism came to be a sterile dogmatism rather than a life *coram Deo*.

In some circles, both in the Lutheran and in the Calvinistic camps, a reaction set in, in the direction of a mysticism. Sometimes we find this in a form that goes back to Aristotle, as Vollenhoven has shown in a most illuminating study of Monarchianism. This particular movement goes back to the monarchians in the averroist movement in the northern Italian universities who, when after the Reformation they were persecuted along with the positive Protestants, fled first to Switzerland, where they tried to penetrate into the Italian refugee-congregations there that were truly Protestant, but from there had to flee to the East (Poland, etc.). There we get Keckermann in Dantzig, and from there the line runs to Maccovius, who was appointed professor at Franeker and was member of the Synod of Dort, and also to Maccovius' pupil, Alsted. Also Burgersdijk (Frans), who in 1620 – the year of the pilgrims – was appointed professor of philosophy at Leyden. One who knows the intellectual history of New England is well acquainted with the role the above-mentioned men played in the history of New England Puritanism.) Third, as the century progressed, so did the awe with which men looked upon the achievements of Reason booked in the new physical sciences (Copernicus, Kepler, Galileo).

There were also a number of major developments in the Reformed camp that lent some authority to the view that there is something in man that is normal, i.e. not under judgment. There is, for instance, Petrus Ramus (1515-1572; converted to Calvinism, 1562 and murdered in the St. Bartholomew's Night). In him we find a preoccupation with logic and rhetoric which is connected with a psychology that goes back to Maruis Victorinus' doctrine of the *freedom of the will*. Ramus' work greatly influenced Arminius, and Ramism became very influential in Remonstrant circles. Again we find a connection with Puritan New England; for along with the men mentioned in the preceding paragraph Ramus was one of the standard authorities there.

The first major breach in the Reformed front was that which resulted from the Arminian or Remonstrant controversy. One can never come to understand what was really happening in this debate when one restricts one's view to the very cautiously worded Theological statement of the Remonstrance. Arminius studied at the new university at Leyden. His learned fellow-townsman and benefactor, Rudolph Snellius, had come from Marbug to reach the Ramist philosophy there.

Another of Arminius' professors at this time, the younger John Kolmann, is reported to have said that high Calvinism (a phrase significant for showing how men thought of Calvinism then!) made God both a tyrant and an executioner. In 1582, because of his signal achievements at Geneva to study under Beza. From there he soon had to move because of his active advocacy of the Ramist philosophy. After a short stay in Basel he returned to Geneva for three years, and from there went to Italy where he heard the great Aristotelian, Zabarella (1532-1589) lecture on philosophy in Padua (1586).

When he returned to the Netherlands he was ordained to the ministry (1588). We are all familiar, I dare say, with the events of the following years, how Arminius was requested to draw up a refutation of the 'latitudinarian' Richard Koornhert and of two infralapsarian ministers of Delft, how in his study of the mater he became more and more inclined to assert the freedom of man and limit the range of God's decrees, and of how the "case" came to a head in the Synod of Dort.

Calvinism had almost become a matter of the acceptance of certain propositions, but life in all is fullness as being lived all around it, it refused to be forced into such narrow confines. From the beginning of the Reformation in the Netherlands there had been a milder Reformation party. A broad, tolerant spirit characterized Leyden from its inception although there were exceptions, like Gomarus. It is the growth of this tolerant spirit that really accounts for Arminius and the Remonstrants. Whereas orthodox Calvinism thought of the majesty and glory of God as the end of man and in him of the whole creation, Arminius and his party were much more concerned with the well-being of men. The Erasmian idea of freedom emerges again in substance in Arminianism. (Compare the congeniality of the Ramist philosophy, based on freedom of the will.) The temper of Arminianism, what may be called its "Humanism" is especially seen, someone has said, in the substitution of the psychological for the dogmatic way of interpreting the Scriptures. This commended itself to many educated minds. It was the temper of Erasmus, of his English friends like Colet and Linacre.

Prof. Dorner of Berlin once wrote:

> …in Arminianism the evangelical material principle fell into the background, and so did the *testimonium Spiritus sancti*. Subjectivity, now no longer inwardly restrained, begins to emancipate itself and to recognize only an external limit in the formal principle (the Holy Scriptures), which are placed in a sort of legal position. Faith, instead of resulting in a living fellowship with God and the possession of salvation, which is involved therein, is resolved into a receiving of the doctrines and commands of positive revelation; and the subjectivity sets

itself to compensate for the loss of the demonstration of the Spirit and of power by proofs for the credibility of the revelation. In this way the reason, with its historical and other methods of proof, and the *fides humana* thereby produced, usurp the place of the *fides divina*. In accordance with this, Arminianism, by its doctrine of the *liberum arbitrium* (free will), allowed somewhat of a Pelagianizing element to enter into the doctrine of salvation and its appropriation…

In opposition to all divine authority in church and tradition, Arminianism will only be bound by the holy Scriptures… But there is shown in its case that if the relatively independent material principle does not, by means of that living need of salvation which it includes, give security for the right meaning and spirit, the exegesis loses its sureness since the subjectivity which is not at once inwardly restrained and set free by the Christian spirit, can easily insert into the Scriptures in reading them what it wants, as well as explain away from them what does not agree with it, and a self-delusion as to unity with the Scriptures is accordingly possible under the title of self-interpretation. That the Scriptures have alone to attest everything is the postulate of Arminianism; but since it will not base the Scriptures upon the authority of the Church, and their claim to authority does not of itself stand sure as an axiom for all, it lays a substructure which is to support and attest the Scripture principle.

But then, as has been said, it is ultimately not the Scriptures, but the *demonstrating* reason, which attests everything. With this end in view, Hugo Grotius already, still more inwardly than outwardly connected with the Arminians, constructed, in his *De veritate religionis christanae* (On the Truth of the Christian Religion), a sort of apologetics for the formal principle, and so did Episcopius (*Episcopii Instit.*, libr. iv., 1.) Arminius himself wrote the *De certitudine theologias* (On certainty in theology)."

The Arminians then tended to believe that the reason of the good man, of the man in earnest about the holy and virtuous life, is the faculty by which the Scriptures are to be interpreted, and the *essentials* of religious doctrine and practice distinguished from the *non-essentials*.

What we have said sufficiently indicates the *tendency* of Arminianism. We know how subordinationist views of the person of Christ (Episcopius) and a governmental theory of the atonement (Grotius) developed, and how the Remonstrant movement merged with the immigrant Socinians from Poland. The importance of Arminianism for our present purposes is enhanced by their close connection with a group of men in England who are known as the Cambridge Platonists because they were connected with Cambridge University.

Most of these Cambridge Platonists had had a Puritan bringing-up. One of the best recent books about them is that by the great German Jewish philosopher who came to this country during the second World War, Ernst Cassirer, *The Platonic Renaissance in England* (Thomas Nelson, 1953). More recently a volume was published by the Cambridge University Press showing the close connection between the Cambridge Platonists and the Remonstrants: R.L. Colie, *Light and Enlightenment*, a study of the Cambridge Platonists and the Dutch Arminians, 1957. What characterizes the teachings of this group of men?

They were moderates, taking up a position midway between the Puritans and the Prelatists. They were pleaders for toleration in the midst of England's civil wars. But what is most characteristic of them is the way they deliberately founded on a philosophical basis their position of tolerance. That philosophic basis is their doctrine of the place of Reason in religion. They subordinate religious conviction to the law of sufficient reason. "Though the human mind is dependent on revelation for the full reality of the saving truths, yet it remains, nevertheless, the measure of their possibility."[11] These men had as their motto Proverbs 20:27: "The spirit of a Man is the Candle of the Lord" but they took that spirit to be Reason. "Reason *discovers* what is Natural; and Reason *receives* what is supernatural", is how one of them puts it. "To go against Reason is to go against God."[12] Cassirer warns us to bear in mind that "That reason upon which they would base religious faith is rather practical reason than theoretical reason. The *a priori* of pure morality is the starting-point of their doctrine; and from here they ascend to religious belief on the one hand, and on the other to the sphere of metaphysical certainty. To speculative knowledge of the nature of the soul and of the intelligible world."[13]

To Puritans and Prelatists alike they say: Unite on essentials and agree to differ on non-essentials. How then does a man distinguish between these two? By improvement of one's reason, by its employment in the fields of science and of moral conduct, and above all, by its employment about the truths of Natural Religion. In this way one grows in knowledge of that which is most knowable of God – a process by which

---

11. Ernst Cassirer, *The Platonic Renaissance in England* (Thomas Nelson, 1953.
12. Quote accredited to Benjamin Whichcote.
13. Cassirer, *The Platonic Renaissance in England*, 41.

one becomes more and more 'like unto God', till the perfection of reason is reached in that 'Divine sagacity" as Henry More calls it, that 'nativity from above', as Whichcote (the founder of the movement) calls it, which makes a man at last a sure judge of what is essential in the teaching of the Scriptures. The Cambridge Platonists go really farther than the Arminians. Reason must be sublimated or deified into 'Divine sagacity' by the presence of God in the soul. The interpreter of inspired Scripture must be himself inspired. "Reason is the divine governor of man's life; it is the very voice of God."

Martineau, in his *Types of Ethical Theory* 211 p. 466 brings out an important point in his discussion of one of these platonists, viz. Ralph Cudworth (1617-1688). He writes:

> The "Intelligible Ideas", then, are eternal and necessary modes of the divine mind; and from the infinite seat they pass into the finite world in two distinct, yet related, ways: by an act of God's Will, things are called into existence of which they become the essences: by a leading of *His Spirit* to centres of dependent being, and communication of *His Consciousness*, they become the intuitive lights of reason and Conscience for all free natures: and this, they guide us, on one line, to the true reading of the universe; and on the other, to the imme-

diate sympathy of God. Hence it is that *all men have the same fundamental ideas, to form the common ground both of intellectual communion and of moral co-operation* (italics mine).

Because religion is reasonable, the 'best thoughts of the best men of all ages and faiths' cannot help but illuminate it.

It is not difficult to see that we are well on our way to the Enlightenment deification of human reason, to its religion of reason, which was nothing more than a pure morality, i.e. morality without religion, and to its confident reliance upon *civic* virtues and *civic* institutions, especially education, characteristic features, all of them, of the thought of Americans like Benjamin Franklin, Tom Paine (author of *The Age of Reason* and *Common Sense*), Ethan Allen (author of *Reason, The Only Oracle of Man*), Joseph Priestley, Benjamin Rush and Elihu Palmer (one of the organizers and the real leader of the Deistical Society of New York). First, however, the Cambridge Platonists undermined the faith of the New England Puritans.

In the first year of the Synod of Dort, 1618, a Scot was appointed professor of divinity at Saumur in France, then the principal seminary of the French Protestants. In his lifetime he also served a Reformed church at Bordeaux and was professor at Montauban, as well as in Glasgow in Scotland. His name is John

Cameron (c. 1579-1625). We may perhaps say that Cameron tried to steer, in some respects, a middle course between the Calvinism of the Synod of Dort and the Arminianism which it condemned. He became a leader of innovation in the Huguenot body. A number of the ablest men of the next generation in the ministry of the French Church followed him, the best known being undoubtedly Mosos Amyraut.

These men taught that "the will of man is determined by the practical judgment of the mind; that the cause of man's doing good or evil proceeds from the knowledge which God infuses into them; and that God does not move the will physically, but only morally, by virtue of its dependence on the judgment of the mind.

The influence of this New Method, as it was called, was felt only a century later in Scotland after it had been developed and moulded by the work of Cameron's followers in France and England. Through Richard Baxter in England the New Method modified powerfully the older Calvinism of Scotland from about the first quarter of the eighteenth century. Baxter also affected the thinking of New England.

Our very cursory survey of the fortunes of 'Calvinism' in Europe has shown us how everywhere, at the critical point, Calvinism's strength was being eaten away by the remnants of the medieval synthesis of faith and reason that were being given new life by the spread of Humanism. The Scholastic scheme of Nature and Supranature found solid lodgment in Protestant thought and Calvinism came to be a body of doctrines to be believed. But life as a whole was coming increasingly to be formed in a paganistic manner. In the Enlightenment of the eighteenth century Rationalism was largely victorious, everywhere except in those inner recesses of the individual Christian's heart where a seed of life was kept alive, partly by the revival movement and pietism. But that was not Calvinism. Therefore it was not the *religion* of the Bible. Only in the Dutch revival of the nineteenth century, in men like the later Guillaume Groen van Prinsterer, Abraham Kuyper, etc. was there a recovery of the meaning of Reformed religion. And this fact is what is behind the tensions that develop so often between Dutch Calvinists and others in other lands who go by the name Calvinist. It has little to do with nationality. In most lands 'Calvinism' has become: arid scholasticism, subjectivism, semi-rationalism, a 'Calvinism' without vigour and ineffectual because men are not united in the service of God in the *whole* of life with a *single* heart.

The Development of Calvinism in North America

We shall deal, very briefly and in succession, with New England Puritanism and the Scottish Presbyterians. I was going to have a section on Canada at the end; I shall have to forego this due to time constraints. Suffice it to say that New England Puritanism was brought to Canada by the Loyalists at the time of our Revolutionary War, and that Scottish Presbyterianism has not been much different in Canada. There is the recent book by H.H. Walsh of McGill University, *The Christian Church in Canada*.

It is used to be said that one of the great mysteries in religious history is the quick deterioration of New England Puritanism. Recently we have begun to be aware of some of the reasons for the sudden collapse. Men like William Warren Sweet, Samuel Morison, Perry Miller, and Joseph Harontunian (*Piety versus Moralism*) have in the last couple of decades added new comprehension to those older events.

First, it is not clear just what the origins of Puritanism are. But it is certain that it did not *originate* with the Marian exiles and the Genevan Reformation. It goes back to the late medieval work of Wyclif and his followers, the Lollards.[14] Into that group, in the course

---

14. See T.C. Hall, *The Religious Background of American Culture*

of time, had entered other influences of a *subjectivistic* nature, like the *Devotio moderna.*

Prof. Haitjema once noted that from 1619 (Synod of Dort) on, the elect and regenerate man received noticeably greater attention, greater than the *Soli Deo Gloria* of genuine Calvinism actually permitted. Certainly this emphasis on the religious experience of the elect received an unwholesome influence in New England from the beginning. Moreover, as early as 1636-38 the Massachusetts Bay Colony was stirred by the Hutchinson affair, when many members of the Boston Church became converts of Mrs. Ann Hutchinson, even some in high station being temporarily captivated by her teaching. Her views were antinomian in that she taught that the inner life of immediate religious experiences is a law unto itself. Another fact worth noting is coming to light: that a close connection, at least in some matters, existed with German Pietism and Count von Zinzendorf.

Many of the standard authorities of the Puritans were Protestant scholastics, like Keckermann and Alsted, rather than Calvin. An intellectualism quickly arose. Predestination was not stressed so much as the doctrine of the covenant, and this was confused with the (secular) idea of contract. It was not long before men were finding their *formulation* of the doctrine more the matter of faith than the great Scriptural verities. There was an almost naïve fascination with Reason, and the logic of Petrus Remus was their tool. Moreover, the formulations were often more after the fashion of the Cambridge Platonists than has, until very recently, been recognized. By the beginning of the eighteenth century, preaching in New England emphasized more the rationality than the personal aspect of God's dealing with men. It is now clear that in New England the theology of Calvin was modified by both English and Dutch forms of Platonism, and that Cambridge Platonism, in particular, was *prevalent* quite early. Even when, at the beginning of the eighteenth century we come to the outstanding and many-sided Jonathan Edwards, we find Cambridge Platonism to be the source of his idealism. In others we find the influence of Berkeleyand Malebranche.

Very early there were charges of latitudinarianism and Arminianism at Harvard University (founded 1636). Just how these are always to be assessed is difficult to determine. But already in the seventeenth century there was a cult of pulpit oratory, which by 1700 we see in a man like Benjamin Colman, a man whose style owed everything to Addison, and who, from his hazy knowledge of Newton, was able to make the statement: "All creatures are Emanations of Overflowing Goodness, and all do continuously subsist by it." Colman set the model for ornamenting sermons with quotations from polite literature, using Plutarch and Milton, but he also brought into his sermons the opinions of men like Archbishop Tillotson. Of Solomon Stoddard, the maternal grandfather of Jonathan Edwards, it was told by a fellow-student that he chose his subject (for a sermon) as though writing an essay worked it out, "and last of all looked for a Text." Sermons were becoming literary orations, to which a text was mechanically prefixed. In 1707 Leverett, Colman's tutor at Harvard, the Brattles (who organized the somewhat revolutionary Brattle Street Church) and Colman captured Harvard College. Colman's moderation, his Addison-like prose style, and his search for a formula of accommodation that would unite all Protestants became the fashion with many Harvard men.

The simple fact is that spirituality had been hard on the decline. It began to be very noticeable after 1660, and in the next decade made great headway. It is well known how, at the beginning, the Puritans required of a man a relation before the congregation of his conversion experience as a condition of church membership. By the time of Solomon Stoddard, the mid-17th century, it appeared that something would have to be done if great masses of the people were not to be excluded

THE DEVELOPMENT OF CALVINISM IN N.AMERICA | 55

from the church. Stoddard decided to abandon the requirement. He declared that all good men, i.e. all who are not of any scandalously immortal behaviour, who comply with the "general moral rules", may and should attend the instituted churches, and even partake of the Lord's Supper, which he regarded as a "converting ordinance." The Synod of 1662 adopted what is known as the *Half-way Covenant*, whereby the children of such "decent" people in the church could be baptized and be regarded as members, though not in full communion. The way of Stoddard, which was more extreme than the Half-way Covenant, became popular. Meanwhile, the doctrines of divine sovereignty, original sin, and justification by faith *were* proclaimed by Stoddard and others as revealed truths. But that is just it. The 'Calvinism' of New England was becoming merely a body of doctrines, to be believed chiefly because it was taught in Scripture. Sermons were preached about the doctrinal content of the faith, but life in the community was something else. The social, economic and political spheres of life, as these developed in an increasingly rationalistic England, were taking possession of men's *lives*.

Jonathan Edwards (1703-58) is a controversial figure. Many Calvinists think of him as a great Calvinist. The fact is that he was influenced by Malebranche,

Berkeley and the Cambridge Platonists, by Locke and Newton, at least as far as the supposed sphere of Nature is concerned. The Great Awakening (1734-35), to which he so greatly contributed was a message of redemption for the individual heart and called for individual fruits of righteousness. Of the patterns of thought at work in the social-economic life of his time, Edwards had nothing to say. Yet New England was very rapidly becoming involved in the ways of the Old World, striving for commercial success, competing for profits, etc. The spirit of European nationalism, capitalism and rationalism with its apparatus of political and legal theory, was growing strong.

In 1722, Edwards, a Yale man, accepted a call to a Scotch Presbyterian Church in New York. In 1708 the colony of Connecticut, following the opinion of Stoddard, had adopted the Saybrook Platform, by which regional associations of ministers were set up. From then on that colony so closely approximated the Presbyterian system that very cordial relations sprung up with the new Presbyterian centers of New York and New Jersey. Again, at the end of his life Edwards served briefly as president of the College of New Jersey, now Princeton University. With him, therefore, we can make the transition to early Presbyterianism in America.

Before the first years of the eighteenth century

we know very little of Presbyterians in the American colonies. The Scottish Presbyterians, who had been encouraged to colonize northern Ireland a century before (the Scotch-Irish), began, under the economical and religious suppression which characterized the beginning of Queen Anne's reign, to undertake a mighty emigration to the American colonies about 1710.

The beginning of the eighteenth century was a critical time for Scotland. Since the Union with England (1707), Deism and Enlightenment ideas generally spread rapidly there. These influences were quickly felt among the Scotch-Irish in Ireland and in the American colonies.

This century also saw a veritable "Scottish Renaissance", which placed the Scottish universities in the very forefront of European culture. Sons of the Church had a great deal to do with it. But, as in other countries, a division arose in the Church between the Evangelicals (who sympathized with the Whitefield revivals and rued the passing of the older Calvinism) and the Moderates (who though nominally orthodox tended to emphasize eloquent preaching, ethnics, natural theology, scholarship and free philosophic inquiry). By the middle of the century the Moderates had gained possession of the universities of Glasgow, Aberdeen and Edinburgh. At this time the Scottish school of philosophy emerges. Of it Sydney Ahlstrom of Yale writes in a recent article:

> ...it is more accurate to see the Scottish philosophers as a liberal vanguard, even as theological revolutionaries, than to preserve the traditional picture of genteel conservatives bringing reason to the service of a decadent orthodoxy.[15]

Jonathan Edwards died in 1758. In 1768, ten years later, John Witherspoon came to America to assume the presidency of the College of New Jersey in Princeton. Though himself an Evangelical, he introduced Thomas Reid (1710-96) and Scottish realism as the tool by which orthodox theology could be defended against Human skepticism, Deism and French revolutionary ideas. In its views on reason, natural theology, conscience, the freedom of the will, and virtue, Scottish realism is a kind of practical rationalism. For that reason it quickly had taken over Harvard's new Divinity School, and had become a part of much early Unitarianism. It had also become the philosophical tool *par excellance* of the New England theology that followed upon Edwards and the Great Awakening, a movement which culminated in Nathaniel William Taylor, professor of theology in Yale Divinity School.

---

15. *Church History*, Sept., 1955.

In the light of the above it is passing strange that it also came to be adopted by Archibald Alexander, the first professor of Princeton Theological Seminary, and by Charles Hodge, his pupil, whose textbook *Systematic Theology* I still used as a main textbook in Westminster Seminary. From Hodge it permeated American Presbyterianism. To quote Ahlstrom once more:

> Consider, for example, Alexander's *Outlines of Moral Science* which Hodge, in lieu of any work on the subject by himself, considered to be the epitome of correct ethical reasoning. Any reader unaware that its author was one of the nation's most inflexible champions of the Old School Calvinism would assume on reading this book by itself, that it was written, perhaps, by some mild English Latitudinarian bent on mediating the views of Butler, Reid and Price. What is important here, though, is that these attitudes brought into Hodge's *Systematic Theology* what one Dutch Calvinist called "the stains of Humanism." The foundations of Hodge's ethic and his conception of natural theology are Scottish rather than Calvinistic.

Ahlstrom points out that in the orthodox seminaries theology "lost its Reformation Bearings". He sees this – I think correctly – as partly attributable to the humanistic orientation of the Hutcheson-Reid tradition.

As this philosophy was adopted, the fervent theocentricity of Calvin was sacrificed… Self-consciousness became the oracle of religious truth… The adoption of the benign and optimistic anthropology of the Scottish Moderates by American Calvinists veiled the very insights into human nature which were a chief strength of Calvin's theology. Scottish Realism accelerated the long trend toward rational theology – a neo-rationalism developed… Reformed theology was thus emptied of its most dynamic element. A kind of rationalistic *rigor mortis* set in.

For the end of the story let me quote Ahlstrom once more:

> In conclusion we may say, therefore, that the profound commitment of orthodox theology to the apologetical keeping of the Scottish Philosophy made traditional doctrines so lifeless and static that a new theological turn was virtually inevitable. Certainly, there is no mystery as to why end-of-century theology in America turned with such enthusiasm to evolutionary idealism, the social gospel, and the "religion of feeling". It was in search of the relevant and the dynamic.

There, in brief, is the whole sad tale. American Calvinism, among the New England Puritans and the Scotch Presbyterians, fell prey to the encroaching apostasy of modern times almost before it got set up.

The rediscovery of the meaning of Reformed religion, as that has been experienced in the revival of Calvinism in the Netherlands, has not been known in America. But that is "the relevant and dynamic" for which American theology turned to the husks mentioned by Ahlstrom.

By God's grace, men like Groen and Kuyper, and those who have followed in their line, have lifted us out of the vast, seemingly inexorable drift of 'Western Christianity' and brought us back to the simple but charged: *Ton Serviteur, Mon Seigneur*. And may those who are participating in this study Conference be deepened in their commitment to work solely for the bringing in of the glorious Kingdom of God through a subjection of themselves and of all things to His most excellent Law. Let us remember that power is the Lord's, and that He works powerfully through those who would serve Him in *singleness* of heart.

ABOUT THE AUTHOR

Howard Evan Runner (1916-2002) graduated with honours from Wheaton College. He earned a Bachelor's degree in theology from Westminster Theological Seminary. He subsequently received an appointment as a junior fellow at Harvard University. After earning a Master's degree in theology at Westminster he traveled to The Free University of Amsterdam where he earned his Ph.D. degree. Runner taught Philosophy at Calvin College from 1951 until his retirement in 1981. He is the author of *The Christian and the World*, *The Relation of the Bible to Learning*, and several other publications collected in the *Walking in the Way of the Word: The Collected Writings of H. Evan Runner*.

PAIDEIA MONOGRAPHS

Other Titles (2020–):

Point Counter Point
H. Evan Runner

The Radical Christian Facing Today's Political Malaise
H. Evan Runner

Christ and Christianity
Herman Bavinck

The Analogical Concepts
Herman Dooyeweerd

The Concept of Sovereignty in Modern Jurisprudence and Political Science
Herman Dooyeweerd

The Criteria of Progressive and Reactionary Tendencies in History
Herman Dooyeweerd

The Secularization of Science
Herman Dooyeweerd

Looking for more?
Visit www.paideiapress.ca

www.ingramcontent.com/pod-product-compliance
Lightning Source LLC
Chambersburg PA
CBHW052030290426
44112CB00014B/2450